REFUGEES

Cath Senker

WAYLAND

First published in 2008 by Wayland

Wayland
338 Euston Road
London NW1 3BH

Wayland Australia
Level 17/207 Kent Street
Sydney NSW 2000

Senior Editor: Claire Shanahan
Designer: Phipps Design
Photo Researcher: Kath Kollberg
Proofreader and Indexer: Jo Kemp

British Library Cataloguing in Publication Data
Senker, Cath
Refugees. - (Global issues ; 1)
1. Refugees - Juvenile literature
I. Title
325.2'1

ISBN 978 0 7502 5434 2

Corbis: Bettman p9, Siphiwe Sibeko/Reuters p15, Howard Davies p 27, David
Bathgate p29. Reuters p25, p28, p38, David Rubinger p32, Peter Turnley p40,
Gideon Mendel p45. Getty Images: The Bridgeman Art Library p8, p14, p20, p16,
cover, Hulton Archive p17, GEOFF ROBINS/AFP p33, p37, cover, MARKKU
ULANDER/AFP p31. Report Digital: Gerry McCann p6. Reuters: p5, p23, p24,
Mian Khursheed MK/JD p32, p34, p42. Rex Features: p4, p11, Sipa Press p12,
p18, p26, Action Press p21,Paula Bronstien p30, p39 Markus Zeffler p10,
CROLLALANZA p33, BRENDAN CORR / The Sunday Times p38.

Printed in China

Wayland is a division of Hachette Children's Books,
an Hachette Livre UK company.
www.hachettelivre.co.uk

Contents

Chapter 1

Who are Refugees?

Refugees are people who have fled their homeland in fear of their life. The legal definition of a refugee, according to the 1951 United Nations Convention (agreement) is someone who has escaped from his or her country and cannot go back because of 'a well-founded fear of being persecuted for reasons of race, religion, nationality, membership of a particular social group or political opinion.'

How many refugees?

In 2007, there were 9.9 million refugees worldwide. The largest groups were Afghans, Iraqis, Sudanese, Somalis,

Congolese and Burundians. In addition, more than 4 million Palestinians remain refugees.

The great majority of refugees have fled from conflict. Most go to the nearest safer country, fleeing from one Less Economically Developed Country (LEDC) to another. Some refugees have to migrate more than once and move through several countries. A minority reach More Economically Developed Countries (MEDCs).

An Iraqi refugee with his two small children outside the single room where the family is sheltering in Amman in Jordan.

1921 The League of Nations first offers help to refugees internationally >>>

1950 The United Nations High Commissioner for Refugees (UNHCR) is established to help European refugees after World War II >>>

1951 UNHCR defines who is a refugee >>>

4

Asylum seekers

Refugees who arrive in MEDCs have to claim asylum – the right to safety in another country. They become asylum seekers. They are not allowed to work until their claim has been accepted. If it is refused, they are supposed to return home, although many remain in the country illegally.

Migrants

Migrants are not the same as refugees, but there may be similarities. Migrants move for a better life. Some of them may be desperately poor, with no chance of a good life in their home country. Chinese migrants, for instance, travel right across Asia and Europe to the UK to escape desperate poverty. Some migrants have fled in fear of persecution

A man in rural Colombia gathers fruit. The conflict in Colombia has been going on for 40 years, and around 200,000 people are displaced each year.

but haven't applied for asylum, so they live as undocumented migrants (illegal immigrants).

Internally Displaced Persons

Internally Displaced Persons (IDPs) are in a similar situation to refugees, but have travelled to another part of their own country rather than crossing a border into another land. In Colombia, for instance, 3–4 million people have had to move since 1985 because of conflict between the government and rebel forces. In 2007, there were about 25 million IDPs in the world – more than double the number of refugees.

 1967 The 1967 Protocol allows the UNHCR to help refugees around the world for an unlimited amount of time >>>

2001 Countries that signed the 1951 Convention confirm their commitment to help refugees >>>

Case Study: Beriwan Ay, a Kurdish refugee

Beriwan Ay is a Kurdish refugee from Turkey. Kurdish people in Turkey suffer terrible persecution (see page 16), so in 1988 the family fled to Germany.

The detention centre in Dungavel, Scotland, where the Ay family were held before being deported to Germany.

Beriwan tells her story

'We came to England in 1999 because the Germans [German government] wanted us to go back to Turkey and we were scared that we wouldn't be safe there. All our relatives have escaped to other countries. Kurdish people cannot live freely in Turkey. We aren't even allowed to keep our Kurdish names but are forced to change them to Turkish names…

'We claimed asylum when we arrived in England and have lived here for four years. Three of them have been very good. All our family was together and we were happy in the house we were living in…

'As an asylum seeker our dad had to sign on once a month at the police station to prove that he was not running away anywhere. But last May they arrested him there…They deported him to Germany and from there he was sent back to Turkey.

'We didn't know what to do when they took my dad so we stayed at home for four days and then immigration [officials] came to take us…We were crying and scared. They took us to Gatwick Detention Centre. Then one day…they told us we were going to Scotland detention centre.

'Most of the officers are bad. Every time they check us they check us like animals; we are humans. My hair keeps falling out and I have been diagnosed with depression; the doctor said I think about things a lot. Our little sister wakes in the night crying out: "Why are we here, when are we going home?"'

Deported to Germany

In 2003, the Ays were deported to Germany. The following year they were told they could stay there for the time being. Then in 2006, their father called from Turkey – he was still alive! Yet although it meant keeping the family apart, he did not want the others to join him in Turkey, where the situation was still troublesome for Kurds.

1988 Beriwan Ay and her family claim asylum in Germany >>>	**1999** The leader of the PKK, which was fighting for an independent Kurdistan, is arrested >>>	**1999** The family travel to the UK >>>

WHAT THE WORLD THINKS...

These are two excerpts from UK publications. Compare and contrast the viewpoints and see if you can find any more newspaper reports or other media discussing Beriwan Ay, her family and their campaign to be allowed to live in the UK.

The National Coalition of Anti-Deportation Campaigns, August 2003

'It is with great sadness that we confirm that Yurdurgal, Beriwan, Newroz, Dilovan and Medya Ay were deported from the UK at 10.00 a.m. on Tuesday 5 August 2003. But their magnificent battle against deportation, which has lasted four years, will continue. We want Beriwan, Newroz, Dilovan, Meyda and their mother brought back to us.'

The National Coalition of Anti-Deportation Campaigns is a UK-based organisation.

David Blunkett, quoted on *BBC News*, Scotland, 16 July 2003

'It is essential that we have properly managed immigration and asylum systems which let into the country only those who are entitled to be here and protect only those who are genuinely fleeing persecution. We are not fortress Britain, but we cannot simply allow everyone who seeks a better life to come here. Where people seek to abuse our immigration controls the government must take the necessary steps to remove them – in some cases, this will include detention.'

David Blunkett is the UK Home Office Minister.

> **2002** Beriwan's dad is deported to Germany and then Turkey >>> | **2002** The rest of the Ay family are placed in detention >>> | **2003** The family are deported to Germany >>> | **2004** The PKK resumes its campaign against the Turkish government >>>

7

Chapter 2

The History of Refugees

For most of human history, people have migrated to find food or better land, or to avoid natural disasters or hostile neighbours. Until the end of the Middle Ages, there were no fixed borders – just natural ones, such as seas and mountains. From around 1500, countries developed strong governments. The European countries were the first to do this. They fixed their borders to mark out their territory. At the same time, a sense of national identity developed in each country. Along with this was a belief that certain minority groups were outsiders and did not belong.

The Huguenots

In the 16th century, for example, France was a Catholic country, following the form of Christianity led by the Pope in Rome. A minority of people, known as Huguenots, were Protestant. They followed this newer form of Christianity that had begun in the 1520s. Ferocious religious wars broke out, during which thousands of Protestants were slain.

This illustration shows the Huguenots being violently pushed out of the French town of Toulouse in 1562, during the Wars of Religion.

| 1492 Spain expels the Jews >>> | 1685 More than 400,000 Huguenots abandon France >>> | 1880s to 1920s 3.5 million Jews leave Russia and eastern Europe >>> | 1939–45 About 60 million people become refugees during World War II >>> |

These Jewish refugee children from Berlin in Germany came to London in August 1939 on the Kindertransport, just days before the outbreak of World War II.

Many fled to Britain, the Netherlands and Switzerland to start a new life. Generally, the Huguenots were treated well in their adopted lands.

Jewish refugees

In contrast, Jews have often not been welcomed. Throughout history, Jewish people have frequently been seen as outsiders and compelled to flee. In the late 19th and early 20th centuries, there was economic and political crisis in Russia and eastern Europe. Some groups blamed the Jews for the problems and launched violent attacks on their communities. In response, more than 3.5 million Jews fled between 1880 and 1929, mostly to the USA and western Europe. From the late 19th century, these countries began to restrict the number of refugees because they were concerned about the numbers arriving.

World War II

The next huge wave of refugees was created during World War II. Around 60 million people were pushed out of their homelands. Many countries refused to take refugees, particularly Jews. Sometimes, children fled alone. In 1938–39, up to 10,000 Jewish refugee children hurriedly left Germany, Austria and Czechoslovakia during a rescue mission called the *Kindertransport*.

Only children were allowed to come. Families in the UK took them into their homes; few of the children ever saw their parents again.

QUOTE >

'The train left Vienna in the early evening. My father placed my small suitcase onto the overhead rack and had to leave the train….Despite the quietly shed tears, the desperate hopelessness of the people left behind was not really grasped by us. The youngest of the children was three years old, and the oldest fourteen. Many children were bewildered as they did not understand why they were leaving their homes and their parents.'

Gerta Ambrozek, quoted in *I Came Alone* by Bertha Leverton and Shmuel Lowensohn, 1990, written about the Kindertransport of 1938–9.

After World War II, many refugees were unable to return home. For example, many Russians did not want to return to a Communist country. Large numbers of Jews had lost their families, homes and livelihoods in the Holocaust and had nowhere to go.

The international community decided to set up a system to help refugees. In 1951, the office of the United Nations High Commissioner for Refugees (UNHCR) was established to assist refugees until they had settled in a new country. The UN Refugee Convention of 1951 defined who was a refugee and what their rights were.

Wars of independence

However, there were further great wars to come. Between the 1940s and 1960s, the African and Asian countries that had been ruled by European nations fought wars of independence against them. Each war led to the flight of refugees. In Algeria, a brutal war between Algerians and their French rulers (1954–62) left a million dead. About 500,000 *pieds noirs* – Europeans who lived in Algeria – fled to France.

People on the move in the southern Rwandan town of Butare, on their way to Burundi to flee from the genocide in 1994.

1945 World War II ends >>>	**1947** The Cold War between USA and USSR begins >>>	**1991** The USSR collapses and the Cold War ends >>>

10

These Afghan refugees living in a refugee camp in Peshawar, Pakistan, in 1995 take classes in a large tent.

Cold War conflicts

Then in the 1970s, there were wars related to the Cold War between the USA and Soviet Union (USSR). These two superpowers fought for influence in other parts of the world, such as Cambodia, Laos and Vietnam. In Vietnam, the USSR backed the Communist government of North Vietnam, while the USA supported its enemy, the government of South Vietnam. In 1975, the Communists won the war. A huge exodus of South Vietnamese people followed.

Civil wars

The conflicts of the 1980s and 1990s created a major flight of refugees in many continents. There were many civil wars, such as in Afghanistan, Rwanda, Somalia and the Balkans. Some wars have continued for many decades. After the USSR invaded Afghanistan in 1979, over 6 million people – one-fifth of the population – were driven from the country. In 2007, the country remained unstable, and 2.1 million Afghans were living as refugees outside their country, mostly in Pakistan and Iran.

 2006 The total number of refugees worldwide equals 9.9 million, 2.4 million of which are in Africa and 3.8 million are in central Asia, south-west Asia, North Africa and the Middle East >>>

Case Study: Slobodan Milosevic, president of Yugoslavia

Slobodan Milosevic was the president of Yugoslavia for 11 years, from 1989 to 2000. At the start, Yugoslavia was one country with six republics, ruled by a central government. In the 1990s, it was torn apart by war and split into different parts. Hundreds of thousands lost their lives.

Milosevic was Serbian. When he became president, he promised to defend the interests of Serbia, the largest and most powerful republic. The Serbs fought two wars against other republics in 1991 and 1992–95. During a third war in Kosovo in 1998, Milosevic's army carried out horrific war crimes. The biggest group living in Kosovo were Albanians. Milosevic wanted to get rid of them to make more room for the Serbs. The Serbian army killed tens of thousands of Kosovar Albanians, and hundreds of thousands

fled Kosovo as refugees. In 1999, NATO bombed the Serbs, and then they left Kosovo.

According to the main Western viewpoint, Milosevic was an aggressive leader who expelled people from their homes. The North Atlantic Treaty Organisation (NATO) was right to go in to stop the Serbs. However, some left-wing observers thought that NATO was wrong to bomb Kosovo.

In 2002, Milosevic was put on trial for crimes against humanity and genocide – trying to wipe out an entire racial group. He died in jail in 2006 before the end of his trial.

Slobodan Milosevic, the former president of Yugoslavia, at his court case. He was arrested in 2001 and put on trial by a United Nations court.

1989 Milosevic becomes president of Yugoslavia >>>	**1991** Serbia takes control of one-third of its neighbour Croatia in a war >>>	**1992–95** War between Serbia and Bosnia >>>

WHAT THE WORLD THINKS...

These are two different publications
commenting on NATO's bombing of Kosovo in
1999. Compare and contrast the viewpoints and
see if you can find any more newspaper reports
or other media discussing President Milosevic
and his treatment of the Kosovars.

NATO & Kosovo Historical Overview, NATO, 15 July 1999

'During 1998, open conflict
between Serbian military and
police forces and Kosovar
Albanian forces resulted in the
deaths of over 1,500 Kosovar
Albanians and forced 400,000
people from their homes.
The international community
became gravely concerned
about the escalating conflict,
its humanitarian consequences,
and the risk of it spreading to
other countries.'

Harold Pinter, The Guardian, 8 April 1999

'Nato's action is ill thought
out, ill considered,
misjudged, miscalculated,
disastrous. It is also totally
illegal....The justification for
the action – "humanitarian
considerations" – is clearly
a very bad joke. It also
demonstrates a profound
hypocrisy on the part of the
US and UK. Sanctions on
Iraq [refusing to trade with
Iraq] – led by those countries
– have killed nearly one
million Iraqi children. That's
genocide for you – in no
uncertain terms.'

Harold Pinter is a British playwright.

1998–99 War between Serbia and Kosovo	**2001** Milosevic is arrested for war crimes
>>>	>>>

13

Chapter 3

Why Refugees Have to Flee

Causes of refugee crises

From looking at history, several causes of refugee crises are clear. The main one is war and civil conflict. These problems are as great today as ever. Perhaps the worst recent crisis in Africa was the five-year war in the Democratic Republic of Congo (DRC) from 1998 to 2003. Government forces – supported by Angola, Namibia and Zimbabwe – fought rebels backed by Uganda and Rwanda. A shocking 4.5 million people lost their lives, mostly through starvation and disease, as well as in the fighting. Around 400,000 Congolese became refugees, and at the peak of the crisis in 2003, around 3.4 million Congolese were displaced. Fighting still continued in eastern DRC in 2007.

In 2007, civil wars between different groups within countries were raging in many countries, including Sudan. In 2003, a major conflict erupted between government-backed forces called the Janjawid and rebel groups in Darfur, western Sudan. The rebels say they are

A Janjawid fighter on horseback in the Darfur region of Sudan. The United Nations has criticised the Sudanese government for failing to protect its citizens from acts of violence by the Janjawid.

fighting because the government neglects them and treats the Arabs of the north better than the black Africans of the south. In return, the Janjawid attacks towns and villages under rebel control, steals from them and kills people. By 2006, around 200,000 had died. Millions had fled their homes in fear. Around 686,000 were refugees, mostly in nearby countries.

No democracy

It is not only conflict that causes people to flee. In some countries, people are persecuted for opposing the government or being members of particular political organisations.

In Zimbabwe, for instance, the president Robert Mugabe wants to stay in control of the country and does not allow criticism. The police use violence against supporters of the main opposition party, the Movement for Democratic Change (MDC). In the mid-2000s, there were terrible economic problems, and Zimbabweans were desperately short of food and fuel. In September 2006, the MDC organised a demonstration about the government's failure to tackle the problems. The riot police disrupted the demonstration, arrested the leaders, beat them up, and probably tortured them.

In 2007, Mugabe arrested the leader of the MDC, Morgan Tsvangirai, and banned demonstrations. Thousands of Zimbabweans rushed to escape the country, many crossing the border to South Africa. They risked being eaten by crocodiles as they crossed the Limpopo River.

Zimbabweans in Johannesburg, South Africa, protesting in 2007 against the arrest of the leader of the MDC in Zimbabwe.

Basic human rights

The Universal Declaration of Human Rights, written in 1948, lists many rights all people should have. The lack of the following rights, among others, may force people to leave their country:

- The right to go to school
- The right to work
- The right to take part in politics
- The right to live in freedom and safety
- The right to be treated equally by the law
- The right not to be punished without a good reason
- The right not to be tortured.

Persecuted ethnic groups

In some countries, particular ethnic minority groups are persecuted. In Turkey for example, about one-fifth of the population is Kurdish. Yet Kurdish people are not treated equally to Turks. In the past, it was illegal for Kurds to speak Kurdish in public, learn in their language at school or to openly practise their culture. From the 1980s, guerrilla groups launched a violent struggle against the government for their rights. Many ordinary people were killed, and hundreds of thousands displaced – most of them Kurds. In the 1990s, about 340,000 people from Turkey applied for asylum in Europe. From 2004, the government began to change the laws about using Kurdish, but the situation has improved little for the Kurds. Many still come to Europe, often illegally, in search of work.

It is not just ethnic minorities who are persecuted. In some countries, it is people from particular religious groups who suffer persecution, or people who are gay or lesbian.

Natural disasters

Sometimes, it is not deliberate human action that causes people to become refugees. Natural disasters such as droughts, floods, earthquakes and hurricanes cause people to run. These problems are always made worse by war though. For example, it is harder during wartime to look after crops. It may be too dangerous to go to the fields. Soldiers are perhaps taking food and water from

Thousands of Kurds celebrating Newroz, the Turkish New Year, in the southern city of Diyarbakir in 2007. At the festival, Kurdish people appealed for more freedom.

A herdsman with his goats and cows in Sudan, where many people rely on livestock for their living.

communities. If there is a drought and the crops do badly, there is a smaller share for everyone. People are likely to go hungry.

The destruction of the environment adds to the difficulties and can itself be a cause of conflict. For example, in Darfur in Sudan, the desert is spreading, covering the soil with sand. Rainfall has been declining over the past 50 years. Arab nomads need grazing land for their animals, while Arab and African settled farmers also need decent land and water supplies. These groups compete for the declining resources. Environmental

problems as well as the conflict push people to move for food and work. Many are displaced within their country, while others migrate as refugees, for example to nearby Chad.

QUOTE >

'We are farmers. But how can we farm here? There's not even enough water to drink. It's a land of death. That's all that it offers us.'

Haroon Ibra Diar, chief of Touloum camp in Chad, which has over 22,000 Darfuri refugees, quoted in *Time*, 10 October 2007.

Case Study: Saddam Hussein, president of Iraq

Saddam Hussein was president of Iraq from 1979 to 2003. He did not allow other political parties, and had many of his enemies put in prison, tortured and killed. Hussein persecuted the Kurds of Iraq and even used chemical weapons to attack their villages. From 1980, he started a war against Iran which dragged on until 1988. At least 1 million people lost their lives, mostly Iranians. Then, in 1990, Saddam Hussein invaded Kuwait, hoping to take over the country's oil reserves.

Victims lying in the road after Saddam Hussein attacked the Kurdish village of Halabjah with chemical weapons in 1988. Around 5,000 Kurds were gassed to death in the attacks.

An international coalition defeated him in the Persian Gulf War of 1990–91 and forced him to withdraw.

During Hussein's rule, many Kurds and others who opposed him left as refugees. In 2003, a US-led military force invaded Iraq, toppled him from power and occupied the country – took control of it.

Since Saddam Hussein's fall, there has been violent conflict between Iraqis and the occupation armies, and between different Iraqi groups. By 2007, somewhere between 74,000 and 1.2 million people had lost their lives. More than 2 million Iraqis had fled as refugees, while 1.7 million had been displaced.

1979 Saddam Hussein becomes president of Iraq >>>	1980–88 Iran-Iraq War >>>	1988 Iraq uses chemical weapons against the Kurdish town of Halabjah >>>	1990 Iraq invades Kuwait >>>

WHAT THE WORLD THINKS...

These are three articles from publications around the world commenting on the crisis in Iraq. Compare and contrast the various viewpoints and see if you can find any more newspaper reports or other media discussing Saddam Hussein and the occupation of Iraq.

Michael Schwartz, Asia Times Online, 8 December 2006

'The American invasion and occupation of Iraq have visited a series of plagues on both the Iraqi and the American people – and on the world as a whole; and these plagues will have no hope of amelioration [improvement] until the US military genuinely withdraws from that country or is expelled.'

Michael Schwartz is Professor of Sociology at the State University of New York and an Iraq expert .

Hamid ali-Alkifaey, 'Voices on Iraq', *Guardian*, 4 Feb 2003

'...since Saddam took over [in 1979], things have changed. At least 4 million have Iraqis have left Iraq, at least 2 million have died, not to mention the non-Iraqis that have been killed, including over a million Iranians, hundreds of Kuwaitis, Egyptians and other nationalities. Saddam has been a disaster for the whole region and removing him is not a luxury. It is a necessity.

Hamid ali-Alkifaey is an Iraqi journalist.

Siamand Banaa, 'Viewpoints Iraq: One Year On', BBC News, 8 April 2004

'The US-led war was the greatest blessing bestowed on Iraq for a very long time. Iraqis can now take the example from the Kurdish region and decide their own future. Our region is one of the most prosperous, most enlightened and one of the most democratic regions in the Middle East.'

Simand Banaa is the UK representative of the Kurdistan Regional Government.

| **1991** Gulf War: an international force attacks Iraq >>> | **2003** US-led forces topple Saddam Hussein >>> | **2005** Saddam is put to death >>> |

19

Chapter 4

The Impact of Refugees

The costs of refugee crises

The human costs of becoming a refugee are enormous. Imagine what it's like having to lose your home and livelihood and to leave your hometown, family and friends behind. You might never see any of them again.

In the panic, some children end up alone. Their parents might even have been killed, right in front of their own eyes – or perhaps they were separated from them during the frantic flight to safety. Lone child refugees might have no one to look after them and be left to fend for themselves. They could be ill or suffering terrible trauma from violence they have witnessed. With no money, they somehow have to find food and shelter. The best they can hope for is to reach a refugee camp, where they will be looked after. Yet they will probably miss out on going to school, maybe for several years.

Some boys in sub-Saharan African countries are forced to become soldiers.

QUOTE >

'I came back from Sunday school and…I saw tanks in front of our house and they began firing….We ran as fast as we could, my mother holding my hand….Feriyo, my friend…fell down while we were still running and there was this deafening noise. I let go of my mother's hand and ran back to help Feriyo but she wouldn't stand up…. I have lots of friends here in my new school in London, and they are all nice but I still remember Feriyo.'

Sado, who fled Somalia when she was eight, quoted in *We Left Because We Had To* by Jill Rutter, 2004.

In May 2003, around 35,000 people fled fighting in the north-eastern province of Ituri in DRC to makeshift camps near Beni, in eastern DRC. Local communities struggled to cope with the large number of IDPs, but were helped by aid agencies.

In African countries in particular, some boys have to become soldiers in order to survive, while girls may have no choice but to become sex workers.

Economic costs

It is impossible to calculate how much refugee crises cost to the country people flee from. As well as suffering the chaos of war, the nation loses large numbers of working people. It is usually the educated and better off who are able to go, while the poorest cannot afford to break free.

The costs for the host country may be significant too. In LEDCs, large numbers of refugees arriving within a short time put a strain on the country's economy and resources. In 2007, there were around 1.4 million Iraqi refugees in Syria and up to 750,000 in Jordan, both LEDCs. These countries received little money from wealthier countries to help them cope with the refugees. In MEDCs, on the other hand, refugees form a very small percentage of the population, so the cost of caring for them is relatively low.

Asylum seekers

At first, it is hard for refugees. In MEDCs, they have to claim asylum. They cannot work until the government has decided if they can stay. Often, they need to learn the language of their new country. It is not easy to fit in straight away and do the job that you used to do in your own country. For instance, many well-educated Afghans had good jobs as teachers or doctors before coming to the USA and UK. Now, many work in low-paid jobs in restaurants or as labourers or taxi drivers.

A young Somali works in his shop in Eastleigh, the area that is home to the majority of Somali refugees in Nairobi.

Richer with refugees

As time goes on though, refugees become part of society. Their children go to school, grow up and contribute to the economy as employers, professionals and workers.

Even in LEDCs where there are large numbers of refugees, the newcomers can bring economic benefits. For instance, Nairobi, the capital of Kenya, is home to up to a quarter of a million refugees.

There are so many Somali refugees in Eastleigh, in Nairobi, that it is known as 'Little Mogadishu' (Mogadishu is the capital of Somalia). The refugees have transformed the economy by setting up as small traders. In one modern shopping centre, Garissa, you can buy everything from designer clothing to electronics. People come from all over Nairobi for the best prices in town.

It is not only the economy that becomes richer. Refugees, like migrants in general, bring new cultural influences. New York City, for instance, hosts many cultures – it was estimated that nearly a quarter of its people in 2006 were born outside the USA. Each year there are huge carnivals to celebrate the various communities. Up to 4 million partygoers join the West Indian carnival to watch parades of people in wild costumes dancing to the music of steel drums, and eat jerk chicken, fried flying fish or rice and peas.

QUOTE >

Clarkston was a small, quiet town of around 7,000 people in Georgia, USA. In the 1980s, refugees started to arrive there. Over the following two decades, the community became one of the most diverse in the country. By 2007, Clarkston was home to people from more than 50 countries, following several different religions.

'There is a Hindu temple, and there are congregations of Vietnamese, Sudanese and Liberian Christians. At the shopping center, American stores have been displaced by Vietnamese, Ethiopian and Eritrean restaurants and a halal butcher. The only hamburger joint in town, City Burger, is run by an Iraqi.'

Warren St. John, *The New York Times*, 2007.

A woman wearing an elaborate costume to take part in the annual West Indian carnival parade in New York, USA.

Case Study: Rigoberta Menchú, campaigner for Mayan rights

Born in 1959 to a Mayan Indian family from Guatemala in Central America, Rigoberta Menchú grew up during the civil war between the Guatemalan government and the Mayan people. The Maya wanted the right to own land, which the government denied them. The long, bloody conflict lasted from 1960 to 1996 and claimed the lives of around 200,000 people, mostly Mayan farmers killed by

During her campaign for the presidency in 2007, Rigoberta said, 'The system has to be changed for the population to receive access to health care, education, work and development. There can be no peace without justice in Guatemala, and no justice without democracy'.

soldiers. In 1979, a death squad kidnapped, tortured and killed Rigoberta's younger brother. The same fate befell her mother the following year. Her father was killed too. In fear of her life, she fled to Mexico in 1981.

In Mexico, Rigoberta joined an international campaign to try to stop the Guatemalan government's brutal fight against Mayan farmers and bring about justice in Guatemala. She published her autobiography in 1983, in which she described the poverty and horrors of her youth. For her work, Rigoberta Menchú received the Nobel Peace Prize in 1992.

Then in 1999, US researcher David Stoll published a book in which he agreed that thousands of Maya, including Rigoberta's family, were killed in the civil war. However, he found that she had altered parts of her story to make it sound more typical of poor farmers' lives and appear more appealing to the Maya guerrilla groups fighting the government. For example, he believed the struggle she described between rich Guatemalans and poor Maya was actually an argument between her parents' families.

Rigoberta Menchú survived the controversy, and in 2007 she attempted to stand in the Guatemalan presidential election, but was unsuccessful.

1959 Rigoberta is born >>>	1979 Her brother is killed >>>	1980 Her parents are killed >>>	1981 Rigoberta flees to Mexico >>>	1983 Her autobiography is published >>>

WHAT THE WORLD THINKS...

These are two extracts from books published by Rigoberta Menchú and David Stoll. Compare and contrast the viewpoints and see if you can find any newspaper reports or other media discussing Rigoberta Menchú and her account of the civil war in Guatemala.

I, Rigoberta Menchú, Rigoberta Menchú, 1983

'My name is Rigoberta Menchú. I am twenty-three years old. This is my testimony. I didn't learn it from a book and I didn't learn it alone. I'd like to stress that it's not only my life, it's also the testimony [true story] of my people. It's hard for me to remember everything that's happened to me in my life since there have been many very bad times, but, yes, moments of joy as well. The important thing is that what has happened to me has happened to many other people too: My story is the story of all poor Guatemalans. My personal experience is the reality of a whole people.'

Rigoberta Menchú and the Story of All Poor Guatemalans, David Stoll, 1999

'When the future Nobel Prize winner told her story in 1982, she reinvented the experience of her village before the war, with the intention to adjust it to the needs of the revolutionary organisation that she had joined. According to her story, the tragic merging of military movements and local vendettas [long and violent disputes between families] was transformed into a popular movement, which, at least in her area, probably never existed.'

1992 She receives the Nobel Peace Prize >>>   **2007** Her attempt to stand for president fails because of lack of money >>>

25

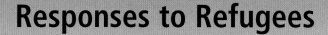

Chapter 5

Responses to Refugees

Emergency!

When war, floods or famine hit, it's an emergency. Waves of refugees run away to the nearest country and are accepted as a group. The host country and the international community provide aid. They set up refugee camps to provide food and shelter.

The majority of refugees move from one LEDC to a neighbouring one. Generally, LEDCs have allowed in large numbers of refugees. Between them, Pakistan and Iran host one-fifth of all the world's refugees. Since 2003, Jordan and Syria have been very generous and taken in around 2 million Iraqi refugees. However, in 2007, these countries began to restrict the entry of refugees. They said they couldn't cope with any more people coming in. The increasing demand for basic resources had led to a surge in the prices of food, water and fuel and the cost of renting a flat. In Syria, many schools had classes of over 60 students.

Reaching richer lands

It is more difficult for refugees to enter MEDCs. Firstly, they are often much further away from major conflict zones. Secondly, immigration laws since the 1980s have restricted the numbers allowed in to Western countries. There are concerns in those societies that too many refugees are arriving. Nevertheless, the proportion of refugees in MEDCs remains small.

These Afghans are hurrying across the border to Pakistan in September 2001. After the terrorist attacks on the USA of 11 September, they knew the USA was going to attack Afghanistan.

Members of a Cambodian refugee family in a detention centre in Australia, waiting to find out if they will be allowed to stay in the country.

The refugees who do reach MEDCs have to apply individually for asylum on arrival. Governments decide whether the asylum seekers have the right to stay according to the 1951 Convention. Yet the law is quite narrow. For instance, people escaping desperate poverty do not count as refugees, even if they would die of hunger if they stayed. In some countries, it is illegal to be gay or lesbian, but the Convention does not include people who have escaped persecution because of their sexuality. Also, it can be hard for refugees to prove that they have a 'well-founded fear of persecution'. Generally, they have to depart in a hurry without passports or any documents at all.

Western countries have brought in measures to try to put off potential refugees. In Australia, all asylum seekers are held in detention centres – like prisons – until their claim is processed. The government argues that this deters people who aren't really refugees from coming to Australia.

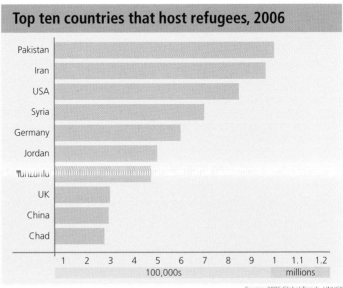

Top ten countries that host refugees, 2006

Pakistan
Iran
USA
Syria
Germany
Jordan
Tanzania
UK
China
Chad

1 2 3 4 5 6 7 8 9 1 1.1 1.2
100,000s   millions

Source: 2006 Global Trends, UNHCR

An anti-immigration poster from the right-wing Swiss People's Party, showing dark-skinned hands grasping for Swiss passports.

Fearing foreigners

The restrictions on refugees have led to a debate in society in MEDCs. Many people express a fear of foreigners and their different cultures and religions. They are scared that if there are large numbers of refugees, they will change the culture of the country. For instance, there is a common belief in Western countries that the Islamic religion, dress and customs are so different from Western customs that Muslims cannot fit into their society.

In addition, some people feel that refugees from completely different backgrounds do not integrate well with the local population. For example, in Australia in 2007, the government cut the number of African refugees it accepted. The immigration minister, Kevin Andrews, said they came from refugee camps in war-torn countries and were poorly educated. It was too much of a challenge to integrate them into Australian society.

Another argument is that there are not enough resources – houses, schools and hospitals – to cope with the newcomers.

Extreme responses

Some far-right political parties have taken up these arguments and say that the arrival of foreign migrants and refugees is one of the biggest problems facing society. They have stoked up hatred of refugees and encouraged verbal and even physical

> **QUOTE >**
>
> 'The gang knew exactly where and when the bus for the asylum seeker and refugee kids would be. I think they had planned it in advance.... It is very worrying that people think they can attack refugee and asylum seekers just because of who they are and where they are from.'
>
> **Abdul**, Algerian refugee in Glasgow, Scotland, quoted on *BBC Scotland* news website, 4 March 2007.

attacks on them. For instance, Abdul is a 17-year-old refugee from war-torn Algeria living in Glasgow. At his school, refugees are generally made to feel welcome – but there are some racists. In 2007, a gang of about 15 boys stabbed him at the bus stop in an organised attack and left him with a punctured lung.

A helping hand

On the other hand, there are many groups and individuals who counter the arguments against refugees. They reason that all societies are a mixture of people from different countries and cultures, and that newcomers should be welcomed. Statistics show that refugees make up a small proportion of the population in Western countries, so they make little difference to the schools, hospitals and homes available. In the USA and Germany, the Western countries with the highest numbers of refugees, refugees formed 2.8 per cent and 0.7 per cent of the population respectively in 2006. Refugee organisations help refugees to settle by providing information on how to find language classes, housing and healthcare. Refugees themselves set up groups to help others from their community.

These Tibetan orphans live as refugees in a children's village in Dharamsala, India. They are provided with Tibetan food, clothes and schooling so they can maintain their culture.

Case Study: UNRWA, helping Palestinian refugees

Around the world, there are many international organisations that help refugees, such as UNHCR, the United Nations Children's Fund (UNICEF) and the International Red Cross .

The United Nations Relief and Works Agency (UNRWA) was founded specifically to help the 750,000 Palestinians who had to leave when the State of Israel was formed in 1948. Over half a century later, its staff still support Palestinians who were unable to return to their homeland –

The Commissioner-General of UNRWA Karen Koning AbuZayd (centre) visits a school in a refugee camp in the Gaza Strip.

and their children and grandchildren. UNRWA provides shelter, healthcare, schools and food aid to more than 4.4 million Palestinians in camps in Jordan, Lebanon, Syria, the West Bank and Gaza Strip.

Those who support UNRWA argue that it is essential because there has been no solution to the Israeli-Palestinian conflict, and the Palestinian refugees cannot return home.

Others claim that UNRWA hinders a solution to the problem because the Palestinians have become dependent on charity. UNRWA has become one of the major employers in the countries where there are Palestinian refugee camps. In 2007, it employed 28,000 Palestinians to run services. The Palestinians rely on the services, while the staff rely on the jobs. They are all dependent on UNRWA. UNRWA is unlikely to work towards a solution that means disbanding itself because so many people would lose their jobs.

| 1949 The United Nations founds UNRWA >>> | 1950 UNRWA begins work helping Palestinian refugees >>> | 1996 UNRWA's base is moved to the Gaza Strip >>> |

WHAT THE WORLD THINKS...

These are two extracts from publications
commenting on the activities of the UNRWA.
Compare and contrast the viewpoints and see if
you can find any more newspaper reports or other
media discussing the organisation.

**Nicole Brackman and Asaf Romirowsky,
Washington Times,
21 June 2007**

'Historically, UNRWA is the main vehicle for
the perpetuation of the focus on the Arab-
Israeli conflict in the United Nations...[It] is
an apparatus [organisation] that maintains
the status quo; the office has no incentive to
develop a resolution of the Palestinian
refugee problem.'

**UNRWA website,
2008**

'Since its establishment, the Agency has delivered its services in times
of relative calm in the Middle East, and in times of hostilities. It has fed,
housed and clothed tens of thousands of fleeing refugees and at the
same time educated and given health care to hundreds of thousands
of young refugees. UNRWA is unique in terms of its long-standing
commitment to one group of refugees and its contributions to the
welfare and human development of four generations of Palestine
refugees. Originally envisaged [planned] as a temporary organisation,
the Agency has gradually adjusted its programmes to meet the changing
needs of the refugees.'

Home at last

Most refugees want to return home if possible. A refugee organisation may offer them help to travel back when it is safe enough to do so. Even if they have no house or job to return to, and life will be difficult, most refugees are keen to go home. In 2007, for instance, tens of thousands of Mauritanians hoped to return to Mauritania after nearly 20 years of living as refugees. This north-western African country has a history of conflict between different ethnic groups of Arab and black African background. In 1989, violence broke out and around 60,000 black Mauritanians fled to neighbouring Senegal and Mali.

Afghan refugees on their way home from a refugee camp near Peshawar in Pakistan in 2002. Between 2002 and October 2007, more than 5 million Afghans returned to their country.

In 2007, the government invited them to return. Sow, the head of N'dioum refugee camp in Senegal, was pleased but nervous about returning: 'We are happy, but we know racism still exists and we will return with fear'.

Refugee resettlement

Some refugee crises, such as the Palestinian situation, continue for decades. The refugees are unable to return to their land and may be allowed to settle in the host country – usually a neighbouring nation. Fewer than 1 per cent of refugees resettle in a third country further away, such as in the West. However, many Western countries do take in a certain number of refugees through a resettlement programme. Since the end of World War II, for example, the USA has resettled thousands of refugees each

By 2005 More than a million refugees return to Bosnia and Herzogovina >>>

Since 2002 At least 300,000 refugees and 4 million IDPs go back to Angola >>>

2005–07 More than 150,000 refugees return to southern Sudan >>>

year (the average since 1980 is 98,000 a year). The Somali Bantu are one such group. They were fiercely persecuted in Somalia during the civil war in the 1990s and fled to refugee camps in Kenya. Somali refugees also persecuted them in the camps. From 2003, around 12,000 Somali Bantu were resettled in 50 US cities.

Non-refoulement

International law includes the principle of non-refoulement. It means that refugees should not be made to return to a country where their lives would be in danger.

In May 2003, this family were among the first group of Somali Bantu to arrive in Phoenix, Arizona, USA. Owing to persecution, they could not return to Somalia.

When their country is safe, they should decide for themselves that they are ready to go home. An international organisation often provides some money or food aid to assist them. Despite the law, sometimes refugees are obliged to go home. In 1995–96, for example, refugee organisations criticised Zaire and Tanzania for forcing back hundreds of thousands of Rwandan refugees even though their country remained unsafe.

| By end 2005 More than 250,000 refugees go home to Liberia after the civil war >>> | By 2006 More than 3.4 million refugees go back to Afghanistan >>> |

Case Study: The Dalai Lama, spiritual leader of Tibet

Born in 1935, the Dalai Lama is the head of the Buddhists in Tibet and their spiritual leader. In 1949, China invaded Tibet and took control, claiming that Tibet was really a part of China. The following year, aged 15, the Dalai Lama became the political ruler of Tibet. He hoped to make peace between China and Tibet, but Chinese rule was harsh. Chinese became the official language, and Tibetan culture was crushed. In 1959, the Tibetan people mounted a mass uprising, but were defeated. Protesters were arrested and killed. The Dalai Lama fled as a refugee to India. He set up a government in exile and continued to lead his people from India.

Since that time, the Dalai Lama has helped to preserve the culture and education of Tibetan refugees. He has led a peaceful international campaign to end Chinese rule over Tibet and promote human rights. Worldwide, he commands great respect, and in 1989 was awarded the Nobel Peace Prize for his work.

In October 2007, the USA honoured the Dalai Lama with a Congressional Gold Medal for his efforts to achieve peace. While on an international speaking tour during the same year, the Dalai Lama commented that Tibetan resistance to China should remain peaceful: 'If we were to use violence, this would endanger peaceful co-existence [living together] in the future.'

The Dalai Lama during an international speaking tour in 2007 that included visits to Australia, New Zealand, Germany and the USA.

Then, in spring 2008, a huge uprising against Chinese rule broke out in Tibet. Protesters poured on to the streets in several Tibetan towns. Chinese armed police opened fire, and the demonstrators fought back. The Chinese government accused the Dalai Lama of leading the protests in order to discredit China in the eyes of the world during the year of the Beijing Olympics. The Dalai Lama denied this charge, saying that he remained committed to finding peace with China.

1935 The Dalai Lama is born >>>	1940 The Dalai Lama is named spiritual leader of Tibet >>>	1949 China invades Tibet >>>	1950 The Dalai Lama becomes ruler of Tibet >>>

WHAT THE WORLD THINKS...

These are three articles from publications commenting on the Dalai Lama. Compare and contrast the various viewpoints and see if you can find any more newspaper reports or other media discussing his efforts and the Tibetan-Chinese conflict.

**Nancy Pelosi,
Voice of America,
28 February 2007**

'His holiness has traveled the world building bridges between and among the different faiths. He has used his position to promote wisdom, compassion and nonviolence as a solution, not only in Tibet, but in other world conflicts.'

Nancy Pelosi is the speaker of the House of Representatives in the USA.
Voice of America is a radio broadcaster in the USA.

**People's Daily,
23 March 2008**

'The so-called "peaceful non-violence" of the Dalai clique is an outright lie from start to end . . . The Dalai Lama is scheming to take the Beijing Olympics hostage to force the Chinese government to make concessions to Tibet independence.'

People's Daily is the main Communist Party newspaper in China.

**Masahiko Komura,
The Japan Times,
17 March 2008**

'I hope all parties involved will deal with this calmly and ensure that the number of those killed and injured does not worsen any further.'

Masahiko Komura is the Japanese Foreign Minister.

1959 After the failed Tibetan uprising against Chinese rule, the Dalai Lama and many other Tibetans flee as refugees to India >>>

1989 The Dalai Lama receives the Nobel Peace Prize >>>

2008 Tibetan uprising breaks out against Chinese rule >>>

Chapter 6

Refugees and the Media

The role of the media

There are many things that influence our opinions. We absorb ideas from our family and friends and from the environment we're brought up in. We are also individuals with our own minds, and may disagree with others around us. The media we watch, read and listen to affect us as well.

You probably have access to several forms of media: television, the Internet, newspapers, magazines and radio. Media with images, especially TV and the Internet, are particularly powerful. Stories with pictures give us immediate and convincing information about an event or issue.

However, the media does not give equal coverage to all the important issues going on in the world. The majority of media companies are owned by large businesses, such as Rupert Murdoch's News Corporation (see pages 42–43). Like all businesses, they aim to make a profit. To do this, they need to sell as many of their newspapers or magazines as possible, or attract large numbers to view their programmes. Many have a strong focus on popular topics, including sport and celebrities, as well as the issues many people see as big problems, such as crime – and refugees.

A bad press for refugees

The issue of refugees is a hot topic in Western countries. Western governments are trying to limit the number of refugees they allow to enter their countries. By talking about refugees as a problem, they have created an atmosphere in which many people feel it is acceptable to criticise refugees. An extreme example is Umberto Bossi, the leader of the Northern League, a right-wing Italian political party that wants to stop refugees from seeking asylum in Italy. He suggested opening fire on their little boats before they reach the Italian coast. The media have picked up on these bad feelings. Stories regularly

> **QUOTE >**
>
> 'After the second or third warning, boom…the cannon roars. Without any beating about the bush. The cannon that blows everyone out of the water. Otherwise this business will never end…Illegal immigrants must be hounded out, either nicely or nastily. Only those with a job contract can enter the country. The others, out!'
>
> **Umberto Bossi**, quoted in *Corriere della Sera*, June 2003.

focus on negative rather than positive things about refugees.

The media are not all-powerful though. Research in the UK has shown that in places where there are no refugees, or very few, people are more likely to believe what they see in the media without thinking about whether it could be biased.

The Internet is a valuable resource, but should be used wisely. When researching sensitive issues such as refugees, it is important to check sources of information and try to make sure they are reliable.

On the other hand, people who know refugees personally are more likely to be sympathetic towards them.

Media hype

To draw people in, media stories sometimes hype up the issues to make them seem sensational. They may be biased and give inaccurate information. For example, they may give the impression that there are larger numbers of refugees than there really are. It's not only the information provided; the kind of language used also matters. Reporters often talk about refugees 'flooding the country' or 'swamping our culture'.

This headline comes from a local newspaper in southern England, after fighting broke out in 1999 between asylum seekers and local youths. The newspaper complained about the number of asylum seekers in Dover, although in fact they formed 0.4 per cent of the population.

These words give the impression that there are vast numbers of people arriving and can increase fears about the newcomers.

A UK report in 2004 monitored the stories about asylum seekers in national newspapers such as *The Sun*, the *News of the World* and the *Daily Mail*. The researchers found that most of them were negative and biased against refugees. The most common headline words used were 'arrested, jailed, guilty, bogus, false, illegal, failed, and rejected.' Through talking to Londoners, the report found that the media stories triggered hostility and even racist attacks against asylum seekers. The report found however that local newspapers tended to be more balanced in their coverage.

Stereotypes

A common problem is the stereotyping of refugees. Stereotypes are ideas about people as a group that are not based on facts, and are usually insulting. For example, the media often portray refugees as 'scroungers' who have come to a Western country to take advantage of the welfare system. It is said that they cause social problems by taking away jobs and homes from local people. There are also stories that say asylum seekers are criminals or bring infectious diseases into a country.

Creating fear

This kind of reporting can make people fearful of refugees. In a survey in France in 2006, for example, people were asked whether they thought that 'large numbers of immigrants and refugees coming into Europe' presented a threat to the continent. Half of them responded that the issue was an important threat, and a fifth that it was an extremely important threat.

Refugees and crime

There is no evidence that an increase in asylum seekers leads to a growth in crime. In fact, asylum seekers are less likely to commit crime than the general population because if they were caught, they would not be allowed to stay in the country. A report by the UK Association of Chief Police Officers states that refugees and asylum seekers are more likely to be victims of crime – they suffer from racist attacks.

Germany has a large number of Turkish immigrants, as seen here. It is also the European country that takes the largest number of refugees. Some refugees in Germany suffer from hate crimes – they are verbally or physically attacked simply because they are different.

Case Study: Rupert Murdoch, the media mogul of News Corporation

Rupert Murdoch is the Australian-born managing director of News Corporation, a global media company that owns newspaper, magazine, book and electronic publishing companies, as well as TV, radio, film, video, production and Internet companies in the UK, Australia and the USA.

Many left-wing people argue that Murdoch's media organisations are responsible for the 'dumbing down' of the media and the end of high-quality journalism and entertainment. Murdoch makes sure that his own right-wing views are spread through his media outlets. For example, Fox News TV in the USA, and *The Sun* in the UK regularly publish negative stories about refugees. They have labelled refugees as cheats who steal resources from local people. Murdoch's critics argue he himself is a cheat. Although he is extremely wealthy, it was shown in 1999 that his companies paid only 6 per cent in taxes, rather than at least 30 per cent like other companies in the UK, Australia and the USA.

Murdoch's defenders say people attack him simply because he is a successful businessman who has made the most of his opportunities. He has brought viewers enormously popular entertainment, such as *The Simpsons* and the film *Titanic*. People have the choice whether to buy his newspapers or watch his media channels.

An image of Rupert Murdoch and his wife, Wendi Deng. In 2008, Murdoch's media company continued to expand. It was announced that News Corporation was planning to launch two English-language satellite TV channels in the Middle East.

1931 Rupert Murdoch is born in Australia >>>	**1950s** He acquires newspapers in Australia >>>	**1969** Murdoch begins to acquire British newspapers >>>	**1973** He starts to buy American newspapers >>>

WHAT THE WORLD THINKS...

These are three articles commenting on Rupert Murdoch and his media company News Corporation. Compare and contrast the viewpoints and see if you can find any more newspaper reports or other media discussing him and his impact on the world's reporting about global issues.

Socialist Worker, 24 June 2000

'The billionaire Australian media baron Rupert Murdoch is an economic migrant. He travels from country to country to make as much profit as he can. He has five homes – three in the US, a luxury penthouse near the Ritz in London, a house in Sydney, Australia – and he owns the Hayman Island. This man uses his vast media empire to label refugees as scroungers. Yet this scrounger has dodged £1.4 billion in British corporation tax since 1988.'

The *Socialist Worker* is a left-wing newspaper.

Andrew Neil, BBC News, 31 July 2002

'Murdoch is "probably the most inventive, the bravest deal-maker the world has ever known".'

Andrew Neil is the former editor of Murdoch's *Sunday Times* and Fox Television News.

Andrew Neil, National Public Radio website NPR.org, 27 June 2007

'I never once got a direct order from Rupert Murdoch that the editorial line of the paper should be a particular line. On the other hand I was never left in any doubt what he thought the editorial line should be. I would regularly get cuttings of *Wall Street Journal* editorials which were taking a sufficiently hard-line Republican [right-wing US political party] line, and they weren't sent just to pass the time...'

Andrew Neil is the former editor of Murdoch's *Sunday Times* and Fox Television News.
National Public Radio is an independent radio broadcaster.

1980s and 1990s Murdoch buys radio, TV, video, film, music and book companies >>> | **1993** He buys Asian media companies >>> | **1996** He launches Fox News Channel >>> | **2005** Murdoch buys Internet company Intermix Media Inc. >>>

43

asylum Protection given to people who have left their country because they were in danger.

asylum seeker A refugee who claims the right to live in safety in another country because of persecution in his or her own country.

autobiography The story of a person's life, written by that person.

civil war A war between groups of people within the same country.

Cold War The hostile relations between the Western powers, led by the USA, and the countries linked to the Soviet Union. It lasted from 1949 to 1990.

communist A political system of government like that in the Soviet Union, where the government controls the production of goods and the running of services.

convention An agreement between countries or leaders.

Dalai Lama The head of the Tibetan Buddhists. The first Dalai Lama lived in the 14th century; the Dalai Lama in the 2000s is the 14th one.

deported When a person is forced to go back to his or her own country.

detention centre A secure place where people are kept, a bit like a prison.

displaced Forced to leave home and move to another part of the country or another country.

ethnic minority A group of people who have a different culture, religion, language or skin colour from most other people in their society.

genocide The attempt to murder everyone from a particular ethnic group.

guerrilla group A group of fighters that make war against a regular army.

halal Meat from an animal that has been killed according to Islamic law.

homeland The country where a person was born.

House of Representatives The larger of the two parts of the Congress (parliament) in the USA. Its members are elected by the people.

humanitarian To do with reducing suffering and improving the conditions in which people live.

illegal immigrant (see undocumented migrant)

immigration The permanent move to another country.

integrate To make people members of society.

Internally Displaced Persons (IDPs) People who have been forced to leave the area where they live and move to a different part of the country.

Islamophobia Fear and hatred of Muslims because of their religion.

Janjawid An Arab nomad force linked to the Sudanese government, which attacks black African villages in Darfur and fights the rebel forces.

Kurd A person from Kurdistan, a region stretching mostly across Iran, Iraq, Turkey. It is not recognised as a country.

League of Nations An organisation formed in 1919, after World War I, which aimed to stop another world conflict. It was replaced in 1946 by the United Nations.

left-wing Describes a person or political party with left-wing views who tends to advocate changes in society in favour of working people.

LEDCs Less Economically Developed Countries are the poorer countries of the world, including the countries of Africa, Asia (except Japan), Latin America and the Caribbean.

Maya A Native American people from southern Mexico, Guatemala and northern Belize.

MEDCs More Economically Developed Countries are the richer countries of the world, including Europe, northern America and Australia.

migrant Someone who moves from one region of their country to another, or to another country.

NATO The North Atlantic Treaty Organisation is a military alliance including the USA and many European countries.

Nobel Peace Prize An important prize awarded each year to a person who has contributed towards world peace.

nomad A member of a group that moves from place to place in search of grazing land for its animals.

non-refoulement Not sending a person back to a country where he or she would be in danger.

occupation Moving into another country and taking control of it using military force.

persecution Treating people badly because of their ethnic group, culture, religious or political beliefs.

prejudice Negative feelings towards a group of people, which are not based on facts.

protocol An extra part added to an agreement.

repatriation Sending someone back to his or her own country.

republic Country ruled by a president. From 1946–99, the republics of Yugoslavia were all ruled by one president.

resettlement To help people to go and live in a new country.

right-wing Describes a person or political party with right-wing views tends to favour keeping society as it is, and supports the economic system in which businesses are run for profit by individuals rather than by the government.

Somali Bantu An ethnic minority group in Somalia that has been persecuted by other Somalis.

Soviet Union (USSR) The Union of Soviet Socialist Republics is the former empire, ruled from Moscow in Russia, which stretched from the Baltic and Black Seas to the Pacific Ocean. It lasted from 1922 to 1991.

stereotype A negative view about a whole group of people, which is not based on facts, for example, 'asylum seekers are scroungers'.

undocumented migrant A person who has not entered the country according to the immigration laws.

UN The United Nations is an organisation founded at the end of World War II, in 1945, to promote peace, security and international co-operation.

UNHCR The United Nations High Commissioner for Refugees is an international organisation set up in 1950 to protect and help refugees.

welfare system A system for giving practical help, such as money or services, to needy people.

BOOKS

Gervelie's Story
by Anthony Robinson and Annemarie Young (Frances Lincoln, 2008)

Give Me Shelter: An Asylum Seeker Anthology
by Tony Bradman (Frances Lincoln, 2007)

Immigrants and Refugees
by Cath Senker (Franklin Watts, 2004)

It Happened to Me: Refugee
by Angela Neustatter (Franklin Watts, 2002)

Jumping to Heaven: Stories about Refugee Children
by Katherine Goode (Wakefield Press, 2004)

Refugees: We Left Because We Had To
by Jill Rutter (Refugee Council, 2004)

Why are People Refugees?
by Cath Senker (Wayland, 2007)

WEBSITES

BBC News
http://news.bbc.co.uk/hi/english/static/in_depth/world/2001/road_to_refug
A report including refugees' stories that looks at why refugees flee, where they go, and how they are treated.

BBC News
http://news.bbc.co.uk/1/hi/world/asia-pacific/country_profiles/4152353.stm#facts
Fact sheet about Tibet

BBC Newsround
http://news.bbc.co.uk/cbbcnews/hi/teachers/citizenship_11_14/subject_areas/human_rights/newsid_1853000/1853538.stm
Information about how people become asylum seekers.

Oxfam
http://www.oxfam.org.uk/education/resources
Oxfam website aimed at ages 8–16. Useful information on Darfur and Iraq.

The Refugee Council
http://www.refugeecouncil.org.uk/gettinginvolved/campaign/campaigners_pack/press_myths.htm
Examples of myths about asylum seekers in the UK press in contrast to the facts.

UNHCR
http://www.unhcr.org
Research, resources, statistics, the main countries refugees travel to and from.